TALK LESS,
COMMUNICATE MORE!

How to Build Connection Through Communication

GERREN POWER

Copyright © 2024 by Gerren Power
All rights reserved.

No part of this publication may be reproduced, distributed, or transmitted in any form or by any means, including photocopying, recording, or other electronic or mechanical methods, without the prior written permission of the publisher, except in the case of brief quotations embodied in critical reviews and certain other noncommercial uses permitted by copyright law. For permission requests, write to the publisher, addressed "Attention: Permissions Coordinator," at the email below.

Published by:
Power Enterprises
gerrenpowerful@gmail.com

This book is a work of non-fiction. While every effort has been made to ensure accuracy, the author and publisher assume no responsibility for errors or omissions. This book is intended to provide helpful and informative material on the subjects discussed. It is sold with the understanding that the author and publisher are not engaged in rendering legal, financial, or other professional services. If expert assistance is required, the services of a competent professional should be sought.

ISBN: 978-1-915922-87-8

Printed in the United States of America
First Edition: July, 2024

For More…..

Follow me on social media!!

TABLE OF CONTENTS

Introduction _____ 1

Chapter 1: Understanding Why it is so Tough to Communicate __ 7

    The Digital Communication Paradox _____ 7

    The Challenges of Being an Introvert _____ 9

    The Challenges of Being an Extrovert _____ 11

    The Challenges of Being an Ambivert _____ 14

    Emotional Intelligence: The Heart of Communication __ 16

    Bridging the Generational Divide _____ 17

    The Critical Role of Listening _____ 18

    Cultural Nuances in Communication _____ 19

    Harnessing Technology Effectively _____ 19

    What Does It Take _____ 20

Chapter 2: The Mind's Subtle Deceptions _____ 22

    How Cognitive Biases Distort Our Dialogues _____ 24

    Strategies for Clearing the Fog _____ 32

    Mastering the Art of Seeing Through Illusions _____ 36

Chapter 3: Breaking the Chains of Fear: Communicating Without Fear of Judgment _____ 39

    Understanding the Fear of Judgment _____ 41

    Factors Contributing to Fear of Judgment _____ 43

    Impact of Not Communicating _____ 44

    Imagining Others' Reactions _____ 46

    Tips for Overcoming Fear _____ 48

Applying Tips in Personal Relationships _____ 53

You Can Overcome it All _____ 54

Chapter 4: Listening Beyond Bias — The Key to Masterful Communication _____ 56

Listen to Understand _____ 58

The Role of Cognitive Biases in Listening _____ 59

Understanding and Adjusting for Biases _____ 60

Principles of Effective Listening _____ 61

Active Engagement _____ 62

Empathetic Listening _____ 63

Benefits of Listening Beyond Bias _____ 65

Improved Understanding _____ 66

Strengthened Relationships _____ 67

Chapter 5: Always Communicate with the End Goal in Mind ___ 68

Setting the Destination _____ 69

Choosing the Right Method _____ 70

Avoiding Misunderstandings _____ 73

The Value of Thinking Before You Speak _____ 76

Adapting Your Approach _____ 78

The Role of Feedback _____ 80

The Power of Purposeful Communication _____ 84

Chapter 6: Overcoming Emotional Communication: Mastering Your Emotions _____ 86

Understanding Emotional Communication _____ 87

Real-Time Examples of Managing Emotions in Conversations __ 96

Building Long-Term Emotional Regulation Skills _____ 99

Mastering Emotional Communication _____104

Chapter 7: The Courage to Communicate_____ 106

The Importance of Courage in Communication _____107

Barriers to Courageous Communication_____109

Building the Courage to Communicate_____114

The Power of Being Vulnerable _____122

Practical Tips for Courageous Communication_____124

The Importance of Putting in the Work_____127

INTRODUCTION

Think about the last time you found yourself in a swirl of misunderstanding—perhaps it was a text taken the wrong way, or a work conversation that veered off course. Such moments highlight a fundamental truth: communication is much more than mere talk. It's an intricate dance of expression, reception, and interpretation, where every step counts and any misstep can lead to a cascade of confusion. In this exploration, we dive deep into the art of communication, unveiling the layers and teaching you how to navigate its complexities with grace and effectiveness.

Effective communication holds the key to unlocking profound personal and professional relationships. It's crucial in shaping our everyday interactions and long-term bonds. In professional settings, clear communication correlates strongly with team efficiency and success, affecting everything from daily operations to strategic decision-making. Conversely, in personal relationships, the clarity and depth of our communication can determine the strength and longevity of our connections. Misunderstandings that stem from poor communication can lead to conflicts, hurt feelings, and estrangement, whereas clear and empathetic dialogue can foster understanding, trust, and closeness. Therefore, understanding the stakes involved in communication helps us appreciate why investing time and effort into developing these skills is not just beneficial but essential for a fulfilling life. Through mastering effective communication, we equip ourselves with the tools not only to navigate challenges but also to build and sustain rewarding relationships.

Further illustrating the importance of these stakes, consider the impact of communication on conflict resolution. Whether in a boardroom or at the family dinner table, the way we express disagreements often determines whether a conflict escalates or is resolved. Effective communicators are skilled at de-escalating tensions by using language that is assertive yet respectful, framing their messages in ways that validate others' perspectives while also expressing their own needs. This delicate balance requires a deep understanding of both verbal and non-verbal cues, illustrating that effective communication is not merely about what is said, but how, when, and why it is said. By developing these skills, individuals not only prevent potential breakdowns but also create an environment where ideas and emotions can be exchanged freely and constructively.

Navigating communication effectively is challenging for several reasons. First, each of us carries a set of cognitive biases—filters through which we interpret the world. These biases can warp our understanding of what others say, leading to distorted interpretations and responses. Moreover, emotions often cloud our judgment. In the heat of the moment, our capacity for rational thought diminishes, and we're more likely to misinterpret others or express ourselves unclearly.

Additionally, our global society requires us to frequently cross cultural and linguistic boundaries, introducing further layers of complexity. Norms and expectations can vary widely from one culture to another, complicating our attempts to connect and collaborate.

Lastly, the digital age has transformed the way we communicate. While technology enables us to connect across distances, it also strips away the nuances of tone and body language, often leading to misunderstandings. Digital communication demands clarity and intentionality to avoid the pitfalls of this reduced context.

Here, we explore how to master the art of communication through a holistic approach. You will learn to recognize and overcome the cognitive biases that skew your perceptions. As we delve into strategies for managing emotions during conversations, ensuring that you can think clearly and respond effectively, even in tense situations.

You'll also discover how to articulate your thoughts and feelings with precision, choosing words that bridge understanding rather than widen gaps. We examine the nuances of non-verbal communication—how to read it in others and use it effectively yourself to add depth to your spoken words.

Furthermore, this exploration helps you navigate the complex terrain of cultural differences, enhancing your ability to communicate in a globally connected world. And in digital communications, you learn techniques to convey your messages clearly and empathetically, preventing the common miscommunications that often occur in emails and texts.

Through practical advice, deep insights, and actionable strategies, you transform not only how you communicate but also how you connect with others. Every chapter builds on the last, layering skills and knowledge that turn complex communication challenges into opportunities for deeper understanding and more effective interaction.

Welcome to your path toward mastering the essential art of communication—a journey that promises to enrich every aspect of your personal and professional life.

CHAPTER 1

Understanding Why it is so Tough to Communicate

Talking is easy; we do it every day without much thought. But true communication, the kind that leaves both parties feeling understood and satisfied, is more akin to art than simple speech. This chapter explores why despite the myriad of ways to connect in our modern world, effective communication remains a challenge for many.

The Digital Communication Paradox

In the age of information, we have more tools at our disposal to communicate than ever before—emails, instant messaging, social media platforms, and video calls. However, these tools often encourage quick, surface-level interactions instead of deep, meaningful exchanges. Each message we send or receive through these platforms competes for our attention, leading to a scattered focus that rarely allows for deep communication.

The convenience of these tools can lead to a reliance on them, often at the expense of more effective, face-to-face interactions. While digital tools can bridge geographic distances, they often lack the ability to convey tone, emotion, and non-verbal cues, all crucial elements of effective communication.

This paradox is evident in our daily lives; while tools like email, texting, and social media platforms provide instant and convenient ways to communicate, they often promote brevity and superficiality over depth and emotional resonance. Digital conversations can lack the nuanced verbal and non-verbal cues—like tone of voice, facial expressions, and body language—that enrich face-to-face interactions. This absence can lead to misunderstandings and a sense of emotional distance among interlocutors. Furthermore, the constant barrage of notifications and the pressure to respond immediately can fragment attention, reduce thoughtful reflection, and diminish the quality of exchanges. As a result, despite being more connected than ever, individuals may feel less understood and less engaged in their interactions, underscoring the paradoxical nature of digital communication in reducing the very connection it seeks to facilitate.

The Challenges of Being an Introvert

For introverts, the internal process of overthinking can create substantial barriers to effective communication. This tendency to ruminate on every possible scenario and potential outcome before speaking can lead to significant delays in response time and, at times, complete communication shutdowns. This overthinking often stems from a fear of being misunderstood or saying something imperfectly, which can exacerbate anxiety in social situations. The pressure to respond promptly in conversations can make this worse, leading to a cycle of anxiety and hesitation that stifles genuine interaction.

Moreover, the struggle with overthinking is compounded by the challenge of not knowing how to communicate effectively in a way that feels authentic and comfortable. Introverts often possess a deep understanding of their thoughts and feelings but may lack the spontaneity or verbal fluency to express these thoughts in the moment. This discrepancy between internal thoughts and external expression can be frustrating and disheartening, making social interactions more daunting and leading to further withdrawal.

The effects of overthinking also extend to decision-making processes, where introverts might delay or avoid decisions due to fears of making the wrong choice or triggering negative outcomes. This indecisiveness can hinder their ability to function smoothly in team settings or under leadership roles that require quick, decisive action. Colleagues and peers might misinterpret this hesitation as a lack of confidence or commitment, rather than understanding it as a thorough, albeit slower, cognitive process.

The Challenges of Being an Extrovert

Extroverts often experience specific communication challenges in social settings due to their outgoing and engaging nature. This enthusiasm to connect and interact can sometimes lead to dominating conversations, where they might unintentionally talk over others or not give enough room for quieter individuals to express their thoughts. This behavior is typically not out of a lack of respect but rather from a genuine desire to share ideas and feelings. Such dynamics can make social gatherings overwhelming for others and sometimes leave extroverts feeling puzzled as to why their attempts to energize the group may not always be well-received.

Moreover, extroverts' reliance on face-to-face interactions for energetic exchanges can become a challenge in situations where such interactions are limited. For example, in settings like casual meet-ups or even family gatherings where many people prefer text-based updates or discussions, extroverts might find it difficult to gauge people's emotions or reactions without the visual and auditory cues they usually rely on. This lack of immediate feedback can be unsettling, as they are used to adjusting their communication style based on the responses they observe in real-time.

Another aspect where extroverts might stumble is in their tendency to process thoughts externally, often thinking out loud. While this can make conversations lively and engaging, it can also lead to misunderstandings if their words are taken as fully formed opinions rather than the thought processes they are. This can sometimes result in hurt feelings or confusion among those who interpret these verbal explorations as definitive statements.

To balance their communication approach, extroverts can benefit from consciously practicing active listening—paying more attention to letting others speak and resisting the urge to fill silences. By focusing more on what others are saying and less on preparing their next point, extroverts can foster deeper and more meaningful interactions. Developing sensitivity to non-verbal cues and learning when to modulate their natural inclination for extended dialogue can also help in maintaining harmonious relationships in their personal life.

The Challenges of Being an Ambivert

Being an ambivert in today's society presents unique challenges, particularly in a world that often seems to favor more distinctly defined personalities—either introvert or extrovert. Ambiverts, who embody qualities of both, can sometimes feel like they don't fully fit into either category, leading to a sense of social ambiguity. In social situations, this can translate to a feeling of being out of step with others, as ambiverts may switch between needing engagement and needing solitude, which can be confusing to friends and acquaintances who expect consistent behavior based on traditional personality stereotypes. This inconsistency can lead to misunderstandings or even to being labeled incorrectly by those around them, impacting social connections and self-perception.

In the professional realm, ambiverts face the challenge of navigating workplace environments that are often designed with either the high-energy, collaborative extrovert in mind, or the quiet, solitary introvert. Modern workplace cultures, especially in industries like tech and creative fields, frequently emphasize teamwork and constant collaboration, expecting employees to participate in an ongoing stream of meetings and group brainstorming sessions. For ambiverts, who may thrive in these settings on some days but find them overwhelming on others, such expectations can lead to burnout and decreased job satisfaction. Finding the right balance and communicating their varying needs for interaction and solitude without appearing inconsistent can be a delicate and stressful endeavor.

Moreover, the rise of social media and digital communication adds another layer of complexity for ambiverts. These platforms often reward extroverted behavior with likes and shares, pushing users toward constant social engagement and self-promotion. Ambiverts, however, might struggle with this expectation, feeling drained by the constant demand for online interaction while also appreciating the connections and networking opportunities that such platforms provide. Balancing their online presence—managing the extroverted demands of frequent posts and interactions with the introverted need for downtime and reflection—can be a constant struggle, leading to feelings of inadequacy or frustration when they cannot keep up with their more extroverted peers. This dichotomy highlights the broader societal challenge of appreciating and accommodating the fluid nature of ambivert personalities in a world that values clear, consistent personal branding.

Emotional Intelligence: The Heart of Communication

Effective communication is deeply tied to emotional intelligence—the ability to understand and manage our emotions and those of others. High emotional intelligence allows for empathy, which is essential in all forms of communication, whether personal or professional. It helps in navigating conflicts, expressing thoughts clearly, and understanding others' perspectives without premature judgment.

However, emotional intelligence is not innate; it develops over time and requires conscious effort to cultivate. Without it, our communications can easily become misunderstandings, leading to frustration and conflict.

Bridging the Generational Divide

Generational differences significantly impact communication styles. Older generations may prefer phone calls and face-to-face meetings, valuing the directness and personal touch they provide. In contrast, younger generations might favor quick texts or emails, praised for their efficiency and convenience. These differing preferences can lead to miscommunications if not properly managed.

To bridge these differences, it is crucial to foster an environment where each generation's communication preferences are respected and accommodated. Encouraging cross-generational dialogue and training can help each group better understand the other's perspectives and preferred communication methods.

The Critical Role of Listening

Listening is perhaps the most underrated skill in communication. Effective listening involves much more than hearing words; it requires active engagement and a genuine attempt to understand the speaker's message. This means not only absorbing what is being said but also paying attention to what is left unsaid—tone, pace, and facial expressions.

Poor listening can lead to a breakdown in communication and is often the root cause of misunderstandings and conflicts. Cultivating good listening skills—through practices like reflective listening and mindfulness—can dramatically improve the quality of our interactions.

Cultural Nuances in Communication

Cultural differences can also pose significant challenges in communication. Each culture has its own norms and values that influence how its members communicate. For example, some cultures value directness and clarity, while others might prioritize politeness and subtlety over straightforwardness.

Understanding these cultural nuances is essential, especially in a globalized world where we are increasingly interacting with people from different cultural backgrounds. Cultural competence—being aware of and sensitive to these differences—can enhance communication and prevent potential conflicts.

Talk Less, Communicate More!

Harnessing Technology Effectively

While technology has made it easier to connect with others, it's essential to use it wisely to enhance communication rather than hinder it. This involves choosing the right medium for the message—for instance, discussing sensitive topics in person rather than via text—and being aware of the limitations of each technological tool.

Balancing technological communication with personal interactions can help maintain the human element essential for truly effective communication. This might mean setting boundaries around technology use or prioritizing face-to-face meetings whenever possible.

What Does It Take

Effective communication is an intricate dance that involves more than just exchanging words. It requires understanding, patience, and a willingness to see the world through another's eyes. By developing our emotional intelligence, embracing generational and cultural differences, and using technology judiciously, we can move beyond mere talk to true communication, enriching our relationships and enhancing our interactions in every sphere of life.

We must learn to equip ourselves with understanding and tools you need to transform your everyday exchanges into opportunities for genuine connection and deep understanding. As we navigate the complexities of human communication, let us strive not just to talk, but to truly communicate.

CHAPTER 2

The Mind's Subtle Deceptions

Cognitive biases are the mind's optical illusions, artfully crafting our perceptions and often misleading us in subtle yet profound ways. Just as a mirage can deceive travelers in a desert, these biases can trick us into seeing reality not as it is, but as we expect it to be. In the realm of communication, these mental shortcuts and distortions play a critical role, shaping how we interpret messages, engage in conversations, and ultimately connect with others. They are the unseen forces that color our dialogues and often lead to misinterpretations and misunderstandings.

These biases are not just trivial quirks of the human mind; they are fundamental to how we process information. From confirmation bias, which filters the information we pay attention to and remember, to the anchoring effect, which ties our thoughts disproportionately to the first piece of information we encounter, these biases can deeply influence our social interactions. They shape our arguments, fuel our disagreements, and even guide our relationships, often without our conscious awareness. Recognizing these biases is crucial for anyone looking to communicate effectively and build genuine connections.

Moreover, understanding cognitive biases can transform the way we interact with the world. It enables us to approach conversations and conflicts with a more critical and open-minded perspective. By identifying and acknowledging these biases, we can take steps to mitigate their effects, leading to more balanced and fruitful interactions. This awareness is not merely academic; it is a practical tool that enhances our ability to navigate the complex social landscapes we encounter daily. It empowers us to break down barriers of misunderstanding and build bridges of genuine understanding, making our social exchanges not only more productive but also more enriching.

How Cognitive Biases Distort Our Dialogues

Confirmation Bias: The Echo Chamber Effect - Just like an echo chamber reflects sound, confirmation bias reinforces our existing beliefs by amplifying information that supports them while diminishing information that contradicts them. During discussions, this can lead us to engage more vigorously with people who agree with us, creating a comfortable but potentially misleading resonance that drowns out alternative viewpoints.

In this scenario, the continuous feedback loop of similar ideas reinforces itself, making it increasingly difficult to break out of established thought patterns. This phenomenon is particularly visible on social media platforms where algorithms tailor content to user preferences, thus feeding them a steady stream of confirming information. Consequently, users may find themselves insulated from diverse perspectives, which can polarize communities and hinder constructive dialogue.

Further, the effect of confirmation bias in stifling alternative viewpoints can lead to decision-making that lacks critical examination. When team meetings or family discussions operate under its influence, they may fail to identify potential flaws or explore novel solutions, settling instead for what feels most familiar and unchallenging. This not only limits the scope of outcomes but also discourages critical thinking and innovation among group members, perpetuating a cycle of mediocrity and missed opportunities. Recognizing and striving to counteract confirmation bias is essential for fostering a culture of open-mindedness and inclusivity, where all voices are heard and considered.

Anchoring Bias: The First Impression Anchor - Anchoring Bias: The First Impression Anchor - Consider how a magician carefully orchestrates the first act of a show to captivate the audience, setting their expectations and focus for the evening. Similarly, in communication, the first piece of information we encounter—much like the magician's opening trick—sets the stage and heavily anchors our subsequent perceptions and decisions. This initial input creates a mental benchmark, just as the magician's first illusion shapes the audience's anticipation and interpretation of the rest of the performance.

Just as a magician uses the first act to direct the audience's attention and frame their expectations, anchoring bias in a discussion can limit the scope of the conversation and skew the evaluation of further information. For example, if a meeting begins with a strong argument pointing out the flaws in a proposal, this negative start serves as the anchor, coloring all following discussions. Participants may find it difficult to see the proposal's potential benefits, as their perceptions have already been shaded by the initial critical viewpoint.

To counteract the anchoring effect, one effective approach is akin to a magician introducing varied and contrasting illusions to provide a fuller display of artistry. In discussions, this can be achieved by deliberately presenting multiple, diverse perspectives early in the conversation. Encouraging contributions that offer different viewpoints or contradict the initial information can help prevent the discussion from being disproportionately swayed by the first piece of information. This method ensures a more balanced evaluation of topics, much as a well-rounded magic show leaves the audience with a richer and more complete entertainment experience.

Negativity Bias: The Dark-Spot Illusion - Just as a small dark spot on a brightly lit wall draws the eye away from the surrounding expanse of white, negativity bias pulls our focus toward negative information, regardless of its relative importance. In social interactions, this means a single negative comment or a minor disagreement can disproportionately affect our mood and perception of an entire conversation or relationship. This bias can obscure the many positive interactions that occur, causing us to dwell on the negative, which in turn can skew our judgment and decision-making processes.

The impact of negativity bias is particularly profound because it taps into our basic evolutionary need to react to potential threats, making negative information more salient than positive. In practical terms, during a performance review, for instance, a few critical comments might overshadow a multitude of compliments. This can lead to feelings of dissatisfaction and demotivation, despite receiving largely positive feedback. In personal relationships, similar dynamics can lead to conflict and misunderstanding, as minor issues are amplified and the overall health of the relationship is underestimated.

Combating negativity bias requires intentional effort to balance the perceived weight of negative and positive information. One effective approach is the practice of gratitude, where actively acknowledging positive aspects in daily life can counterbalance the psychological impact of negative experiences. Additionally, cultivating a habit of giving equal voice to positive developments or feedback during discussions can help mitigate the bias's effects. Encouraging more balanced perceptions helps us maintain a more accurate and healthy perspective on our interactions and overall life circumstances.

Predetermined Bias: The Rear View Mirror Effect - Predetermined bias in personal and romantic relationships can have a profound impact, shaping the way one perceives and interacts with a partner, often based on past experiences or ingrained stereotypes. This type of bias can manifest when one enters a new relationship carrying expectations or judgments formed from previous partnerships. For instance, if someone has been in a relationship where communication was poor, they might preemptively expect or interpret their new partner's actions through a lens of suspicion or doubt, potentially accusing them of withholding information or being uncommunicative, even when such behaviors have not occurred.

These biases can also influence how one perceives compatibility and relationship dynamics. For example, societal or cultural norms might lead someone to believe that a successful relationship must follow certain patterns or roles. If a new relationship deviates from these patterns—such as having a partner who expresses emotions differently than expected—it may lead to dissatisfaction or misunderstandings, not necessarily because the relationship is flawed, but because it doesn't fit the preconceived mold.

To counteract these biases, it is essential for individuals to engage in self-reflection and open dialogue. Recognizing one's own biases can be challenging but is crucial in fostering healthier and more understanding relationships. Couples should strive to communicate their expectations and experiences openly, discussing how their past might influence their present interactions without judgment. This can help both partners understand each other's perspectives more deeply and work together to overcome biases, ensuring they respond to each other's actions based on the present reality rather than past experiences. Building such mutual understanding and empathy can significantly mitigate the negative effects of predetermined biases, allowing relationships to flourish based on genuine interaction and mutual respect.

Strategies for Clearing the Fog

Expanding the Field of View: Embracing Diverse Perspectives

To combat the narrowing effects of cognitive biases, it's essential to consciously widen our mental lens, allowing us to absorb a broader range of perspectives. This involves actively seeking out viewpoints that differ from our own, especially those that challenge our preconceived notions. In practice, this can mean inviting input from individuals who come from different backgrounds or have unique experiences. Encouraging diversity of thought in discussions helps to check our biases and prevents us from falling into the echo chambers that reinforce them. Such an approach not only enriches our understanding but also cultivates a more inclusive environment where all voices are heard and valued.

Moreover, fostering an environment where questioning is encouraged can further expand our field of view. Asking probing questions and encouraging others to do the same can uncover assumptions and biases that might otherwise go unchallenged. This method of engaging with diverse perspectives ensures a more thorough vetting of ideas and promotes a culture where critical thinking is the norm, helping to dismantle the barriers erected by unchecked biases.

Adjusting the Focus: Pausing to Reflect

Implementing a moment of reflection before forming judgments or making decisions is a powerful antidote to the rush to conclusion that biases often provoke. This pause allows for a deeper processing of information, enabling us to weigh additional data and consider alternative interpretations. Such a reflective practice can be as simple as taking a brief pause in conversation to consider the other person's viewpoint or delaying a decision until all facts have been reviewed. By slowing down our thought processes, we give ourselves the space to identify and adjust for biases such as anchoring or confirmation bias, leading to more thoughtful and less reactive responses.

This reflective pause also aids in reducing the impact of emotional reactions, which can be heightened by biases like the negativity bias. By allowing ourselves time to process our emotional responses, we can respond from a place of reason rather than reaction. This strategy not only helps in personal interactions but also enhances our ability to navigate complex professional landscapes where calm deliberation is often necessary.

Incorporating New Angles: Fostering a Culture of Openness and Humor

Introducing humor and openness into discussions can significantly lighten the atmosphere, making it easier to address and adjust for cognitive biases. When we can laugh at ourselves and the mistakes we make, it reduces the stigma associated with errors in judgment, making it easier to admit and correct them. This approach not only makes interactions more pleasant but also more productive, as people feel safe to express unconventional ideas or challenge the status quo without fear of ridicule or reprisal.

Creating a culture where cognitive biases are openly discussed and humorously explored can demystify these often-invisible influences, making them more recognizable and easier to manage. Encouraging team members or conversation partners to share instances

where they noticed their biases impacting their decisions can foster an environment of learning and growth. This transparency not only builds trust but also enhances collective understanding, equipping everyone with the tools to better identify and counteract biases in their thinking and communication.

Mastering the Art of Seeing Through Illusions

By understanding and addressing cognitive biases, we can begin to clear the fog that these mental illusions cast over our communications. Just as understanding the tricks behind an optical illusion can prevent us from being fooled, understanding our cognitive biases can prevent us from falling into communication traps. This knowledge empowers us to have richer, more balanced conversations and to build stronger, more understanding relationships. It turns the challenge of navigating cognitive biases into an opportunity for growth and learning, transforming potential misunderstandings into moments of connection and insight.

When we interact with others, our minds often play tricks on us, much like a magician using sleight of hand. For instance, the 'confirmation bias' leads us to pay more attention to information that supports our beliefs and ignore what doesn't. It's like having a pair of glasses that only shows us what we want to see. By recognizing this bias, we can start to remove these glasses and see the world and other people more clearly. This clarity allows us to engage in conversations that are not only more honest and open but also more enriching and fulfilling.

Similarly, the 'bandwagon effect' is another illusion where we tend to agree with opinions or take actions because many other people do, even if it's not the best choice. Imagine you're at a concert, and everyone starts clapping before a performance has ended; you might feel compelled to join in, even if you think it's too early. Recognizing this effect helps us to stand firm in our own perceptions and decisions, fostering more genuine interactions. By learning to identify and manage such biases, we transform every conversation into a stepping stone towards deeper understanding and mutual respect.

CHAPTER 3

Breaking the Chains of Fear: Communicating Without Fear of Judgment

The fear of judgment is a powerful force that can significantly hinder our ability to communicate effectively. Many people experience this fear, whether in a classroom, at work, or in personal relationships. It's not just about missing the chance to speak up; it's about missing the opportunity to connect, share, and grow. This chapter will explore the roots of this fear, its far-reaching impacts, and practical strategies to overcome it, enabling you to become a more confident and effective communicator.

Humans are inherently social creatures, driven by a deep-seated need for acceptance and belonging. From an early age, we learn the importance of fitting in and being liked by others. This need for acceptance can sometimes overshadow our desire to express ourselves honestly and openly. Imagine being in a small boat during a storm. Instead of steering the boat, you let the waves toss you around. Similarly, when we allow the fear of judgment to control our communication, we give away our power to others' potential reactions. This fear can manifest in various ways, from not sharing our true feelings with a partner to avoiding speaking up in a work meeting.

However, overcoming this fear is essential for personal and professional growth. Effective communication is the key to building strong relationships, solving problems, and achieving success. When we communicate openly, we can share our ideas, express our feelings, and build trust with those around us. By understanding the origins of our fear and learning how to manage it, we can break free from the chains that hold us back and unlock our full potential as communicators. In the following sections, we will explore the factors that contribute to this fear, its impact on our lives, and strategies to overcome it.

Understanding the Fear of Judgment

The fear of what others will think is deeply ingrained in our desire for social acceptance. From an early age, humans are conditioned to seek validation and approval from those around us. This desire for social acceptance is a natural part of being human, as it ensures that we fit into social groups, which historically has been crucial for survival. However, this need for acceptance can sometimes overshadow our desire to express ourselves honestly and openly. When we prioritize others' opinions over our own voice, we limit our ability to communicate effectively and authentically.

This fear of judgment often stems from past experiences where we might have been criticized, ridiculed, or dismissed for expressing our thoughts and feelings. Such negative encounters can leave lasting impressions, leading us to anticipate similar reactions in future interactions. Over time, this anticipation becomes internalized, and we start censoring ourselves to avoid potential criticism. This self-censorship not only hampers our ability to communicate but also affects our self-esteem and self-worth. We start doubting the value of our contributions and become increasingly reliant on external validation, thus perpetuating the cycle of fear.

When we allow the fear of judgment to control our communication, we essentially give away our power to others' potential reactions. We start imagining worst-case scenarios and assume that others will react negatively to our words, even without any concrete evidence. This habit of mind-reading can be particularly detrimental, as it prevents us from speaking our truth and engaging in meaningful conversations. By assuming what others might think or say, we rob them of the opportunity to respond authentically. This not only stifles open dialogue but also creates barriers to genuine connection and understanding. To overcome this, it is essential to recognize these fears, challenge our assumptions, and gradually build the confidence to express ourselves without the constant worry of judgment.

Factors Contributing to Fear of Judgment

One significant factor contributing to the fear of judgment is past experiences. If you've ever been mocked or harshly criticized for sharing your thoughts, it's natural to want to avoid that kind of pain again. These negative experiences can create a lingering fear that re-emerges whenever we consider speaking up. Another crucial factor is low self-esteem. When we lack confidence in our worth or abilities, we are more likely to believe that others will also undervalue our contributions. This lack of self-belief can be a substantial barrier to effective communication.

Perceived expectations also play a significant role. Often, we imagine that others have very high expectations of us, and we fear that our ideas or feelings won't measure up. This imagined pressure can be paralyzing, making it difficult to express ourselves freely. Additionally, social anxiety can exacerbate the fear of negative evaluation by others. Feeling anxious in social situations can make us overly concerned about how we are perceived, further inhibiting our ability to communicate openly and confidently.

Impact of Not Communicating

When we choose not to communicate because of fear, the consequences can be profound and far-reaching. It's akin to holding a key to a treasure chest but being too afraid to use it. One of the most significant impacts is missed opportunities. When ideas remain unheard, potential contributions are lost, and we miss the chance to make a positive impact. This can be especially detrimental in group settings where collaboration and diverse ideas are essential for success.

Lack of communication can also lead to misunderstandings and strained relationships. When we don't express our thoughts and feelings, others may misinterpret our silence, leading to conflicts and misunderstandings. Over time, these misunderstandings can erode trust and weaken relationships. Furthermore, not communicating can hinder personal growth. By not expressing ourselves, we miss opportunities to receive feedback and learn from others, which is essential for personal development.

Increased stress is another consequence of not communicating. Bottling up thoughts and feelings can lead to emotional turmoil and stress, which can negatively affect our mental and physical health. Chronic stress can contribute to a host of health problems, including anxiety, depression, and heart disease. It's important to recognize these impacts and understand that by not communicating, we are limiting ourselves in many ways.

Imagining Others' Reactions

One of the most common pitfalls in communication is assuming how others will react to what we say. This habit of preemptively deciding others' thoughts can significantly hinder genuine interaction. When we anticipate negative reactions, we often project our own insecurities and fears onto others. This can lead us to remain silent or alter our message in ways that are not authentic. By imagining negative responses, we create a self-fulfilling prophecy where our fears dictate our actions, thus robbing us of genuine connection and understanding.

Moreover, when we assume we know what others are thinking, we deny them the opportunity to share their actual thoughts and feelings. This can be particularly damaging in personal relationships. For instance, if you assume your partner will dismiss your feelings about a particular issue, you might choose not to bring it up at all. This not only prevents resolution but also builds a barrier of unspoken issues that can accumulate over time, creating distance and resentment. By not giving others the chance to respond, we miss out on potential support, empathy, and solutions that could strengthen the relationship.

Imagining others' reactions can also lead to a form of mind-reading where we believe we understand others' thoughts without actually asking them. This can create significant misunderstandings. For example, if a friend seems distant, you might assume they are upset with you without verifying this assumption. Your subsequent actions based on this false belief can strain the friendship further. Direct communication, where we ask and clarify rather than assume, is essential. By doing so, we open the door to honest dialogue and mutual understanding, rather than letting imagined scenarios control our interactions.

Tips for Overcoming Fear

Overcoming the fear of judgment is like learning to ride a bike. At first, it feels scary, but with practice, it becomes easier. Here are some tips to help you overcome this fear:

Recognize Your Value: Understand that your thoughts and ideas are valuable. Everyone has unique perspectives to offer. Remind yourself that your voice matters and that you have something important to contribute. Recognizing your own value is the first step towards building confidence in your ability to communicate.

Start Small: Begin by sharing your thoughts in less intimidating situations, like with close friends or family. Gradually work your way up to larger groups and more formal settings. This can help build your confidence and make it easier to communicate openly. Starting small allows you to gain positive experiences and gradually reduce your fear of judgment.

Focus on the Positive: Remember past experiences where speaking up led to positive outcomes. Reflect on times when your contributions were appreciated and made a difference. This can help reinforce the benefits of communicating and reduce your fear of judgment. By focusing on positive experiences, you can shift your mindset and build a more positive outlook on communication.

Prepare and Practice: If you need to communicate something important, prepare in advance and practice what you want to say. This can help you feel more confident and reduce anxiety. Consider writing down your thoughts or talk to a trusted friend or family member. Preparation and practice can help you organize your thoughts and deliver your message more effectively.

Challenge Negative Thoughts: When you catch yourself fearing judgment, challenge those thoughts. Ask yourself if they are realistic or just assumptions. Remind yourself that others are likely more focused on their own thoughts and feelings than on judging you. Challenging negative thoughts can help you gain perspective and reduce irrational fears.

Seek Support: Surround yourself with supportive people who encourage open communication. Seek out friends, family members, or mentors who can provide positive feedback and help you build your confidence. Having a support system can make a significant difference in overcoming fear and building confidence.

Use Analogies: Just like planting a seed can grow into a beautiful tree, sharing your thoughts can lead to great ideas and solutions. Use analogies to help you visualize the positive outcomes of communicating and to remind yourself that your contributions can have a significant impact. Analogies can make abstract concepts more relatable and help you understand the importance of communication.

Visualize Success: Visualization can be a powerful tool. Take a few minutes each day to visualize yourself speaking confidently and being well-received by others. Imagine positive scenarios where your contributions are valued and appreciated. Visualization can help you build a positive mental image of yourself as a confident communicator.

Set Realistic Goals: Set small, achievable goals for yourself when it comes to communication. For example, aim to speak up at least once in every meeting or to share one new idea each week. Setting realistic goals can help you gradually build confidence and reduce fear. Celebrate your successes along the way to reinforce positive behavior.

Mindfulness and Relaxation Techniques: Practicing mindfulness and relaxation techniques can help reduce anxiety and stress. Techniques such as deep breathing, meditation, and progressive muscle relaxation can help you stay calm and focused in social situations. Incorporating these practices into your daily routine can improve your overall well-being and communication skills.

Reflect on Feedback: When you do receive feedback, take time to reflect on it constructively. Instead of viewing criticism as a negative judgment, see it as an opportunity for growth and improvement. Constructive feedback can provide valuable insights and help you become a better communicator.

Embrace Mistakes: Understand that everyone makes mistakes, and they are a natural part of the learning process. Don't be too hard on yourself if things don't go perfectly. Embrace mistakes as opportunities to learn and grow. Remember that even experienced communicators have moments of doubt and imperfection.

Applying Tips in Personal Relationships

These tips are not only useful in professional or academic settings but also vital for personal relationships. For instance, in friendships, recognizing your value can help you voice your concerns without fear of being dismissed. In the case of Emily and Lisa, had Emily acknowledged her worth and the importance of her feelings, she might have felt more confident in expressing her concerns about their friendship. Starting small by having casual conversations about feelings can pave the way for more significant discussions.

In romantic relationships, focusing on the positive and practicing mindful communication can make a significant difference. For Mark and Jennifer, if Mark had taken time to reflect on positive past conversations and practiced how to express his feelings calmly and clearly, he might have been more inclined to communicate his needs without fear. Using analogies, like explaining that their relationship is like a garden that needs regular care and attention, can also help make the conversation more relatable and less confrontational.

You Can Overcome it All

Fear of judgment and imagining how others might react are common barriers to effective communication, but they don't have to hold you back. By understanding why these fears exist and taking steps to overcome them, you can unlock your full potential as a communicator. Remember, your voice matters. Every time you speak up, you are steering your own boat, guiding it towards new opportunities and growth. Don't let fear

Talk Less, Communicate More!

keep you anchored in silence. Speak up, share your thoughts, and watch as your world expands with possibilities.

CHAPTER 4

Listening Beyond Bias — The Key to Masterful Communication

Mastering effective communication is akin to being an excellent DJ at a party; you need to listen to the room, understand the mood, and adjust your playlist accordingly. Effective listening isn't just about hearing words; it's about understanding the deeper melodies of emotions and thoughts behind those words. To reach this level of communication mastery, one must first address and manage their own cognitive biases, those mental filters that can distort perceptions and hinder authentic interactions.

Additionally, mastering effective communication, much like being a savvy DJ, involves more than just playing the right tracks; it requires a keen sense of timing and adaptation. A good DJ wouldn't stick to a set playlist if the crowd isn't feeling the vibe. Similarly, a proficient communicator must be flexible, ready to shift their approach based on the feedback received during the interaction. Cognitive biases can be likened to wearing noise-canceling headphones at a live event—you might miss out on the crowd's reaction and the ambient atmosphere that's crucial for truly connecting. Addressing your biases helps strip away the layers of distortion, enabling you to tune into the subtle emotional shifts and unspoken thoughts of your conversational partners, ensuring the communication flows as smoothly and impactfully as the music at a great party.

Listen to Understand

Listening to understand rather than just to respond, especially when you disagree, is akin to playing in a band. In a musical band, each member must listen carefully to the others to ensure their sounds blend harmoniously. Similarly, when you listen with the intent to understand, you are paying close attention to the other person's verbal and emotional notes, integrating them into your own response. This doesn't mean you have to agree with everything they say, but it means you are genuinely engaging with their perspective, allowing for a more symphonic exchange of ideas. Just as band members must coordinate their rhythms and melodies, effective communication requires aligning your understanding with the speaker's intentions, fostering cooperation even amid differing viewpoints.

On the other hand, listening only to speak is like a band member playing out of turn or ignoring the tune that the rest of the group is following. This can disrupt the musical harmony, leading to a disjointed performance. In conversations, if you're simply waiting for your chance to speak, you might overlook key elements of the other person's message, which can lead to misunderstandings and friction. By prioritizing listening to understand, you promote a dialogue that is more like a well-rehearsed musical piece, where each participant's contributions are valued and the overall communication is more effective and resonant. This approach ensures that everyone feels heard and respected, creating a richer, more engaging interaction.

The Role of Cognitive Biases in Listening

Cognitive biases can be thought of as mental noise that distorts clear communication. They're like the buzz in old radio speakers that can drown out the music you're trying to enjoy. For instance, confirmation bias might make you tune into information that resonates with your existing beliefs and tune out dissenting voices. It's like having a radio that only picks up your favorite stations, ignoring all others regardless of their potential value.

Overcoming these biases begins with recognizing them, like realizing that your radio isn't picking up all the available stations. Once you know your reception is limited, you can start adjusting the settings. Awareness is the first step toward clearer, more inclusive listening, where you're open to receiving all signals, not just the ones you prefer.

Understanding and Adjusting for Biases

Gaining an understanding of your biases is akin to understanding why you like certain music genres but not others. This self-awareness helps you realize how your preferences might limit your enjoyment of other types of music. When you apply this awareness to listening in conversations, it encourages you to mentally step back and question whether your internal 'listener' is being selective based on old habits.

Adjusting for these biases involves actively choosing to change the station, to continue with our radio analogy. It's about deciding to explore other genres of thought or perspectives that you might typically ignore. This adjustment doesn't just broaden your auditory range; it enriches your communicative experiences, allowing for more diverse and inclusive interactions.

Principles of Effective Listening

Effective listening is about much more than just not talking while the other person speaks. It's about fully engaging with the speaker, entering their emotional and intellectual space, and experiencing the conversation as a dynamic exchange of ideas.

Moreover, effective listening involves an intuitive sense of the conversation's flow and energy. It's about actively participating in the dialogue through attentive silence and thoughtful responses. Think of it as being a conductor in an orchestra where each pause, each breath taken by the musicians, contributes to the performance's overall impact. In conversations, these moments of silence are opportunities to connect deeper, allowing the speaker to gather thoughts or emphasize a point. By respecting these spaces and responding thoughtfully, you ensure the dialogue is not just an exchange of words but a meaningful and collaborative journey of understanding.

Active Engagement

Active engagement in listening is like dancing to the rhythm of the conversation. It requires you to be present in the moment, responding to the speaker's verbal and non-verbal cues. This means maintaining eye contact, nodding in understanding, and perhaps interjecting with thoughtful affirmations or questions that show you are tuned in and genuinely interested.

Listening involves synchronizing with the speaker's emotional state and adjusting your reactions accordingly. It's similar to how a dancer feels the music and alters their movements to match the tempo and mood. By being attuned to changes in the speaker's tone, pace, and body language, you can respond more empathetically and effectively. This might mean softening your voice to match a delicate subject, or mirroring the speaker's enthusiasm when they share something exciting. Such attentiveness not only enhances the connection but also deepens the mutual respect and understanding within the conversation.

Empathetic Listening

Empathy in listening is trying to feel the music the way the speaker feels it, not just listening to the notes but absorbing the emotion and intention behind them. It's about understanding the context of their words and connecting on a human level, which can transform a simple exchange of words into a meaningful interaction.

Develop the ability to acknowledge the speaker's emotions without judgment, allowing them to express themselves freely and fully. This type of listening is like tuning into a song not just for its melody but for its emotional resonance, understanding the heartache in a blues riff or the joy in an upbeat chorus. By validating the speaker's feelings and offering a space where they feel heard and understood, you build a deeper rapport. This connection facilitates a more genuine dialogue where both parties feel safe to share openly and honestly, enhancing the quality and depth of the interaction significantly.

Benefits of Listening Beyond Bias

Listening without bias doesn't just clear the static from the conversation; it amplifies its quality and can profoundly affect both personal and professional relationships.

Listening without bias also enhances the authenticity of your interactions. When you remove your own filters and truly listen, you communicate to others that their viewpoints matter, creating an environment of trust and openness. This kind of genuine engagement encourages others to express themselves more freely and fully, knowing they will be heard without immediate critique or dismissal. As a result, conversations become more dynamic and substantial, leading to stronger bonds and more effective collaboration in both personal and professional contexts.

Improved Understanding

By tuning into the true essence of what is being communicated, you capture the full spectrum of the conversation. This comprehensive understanding allows for better responses, smarter decisions, and more effective problem-solving. It's like finally hearing the bass line that completes the song, filling out the sound and enriching the entire listening experience.

Moreover, by delving into the full depth of the conversation, you foster a richer dialogue where nuanced opinions and subtle cues become clear. This kind of deep listening allows for a more layered understanding of the issues at hand, which can lead to breakthroughs in complex problem-solving scenarios. It's akin to an artist who sees not just the primary colors but the myriad of shades in between; this detailed perception enables more refined and nuanced responses. Such thorough engagement ensures that decisions are not just reactive but are well-informed and thoughtfully considered, enhancing the effectiveness and sustainability of solutions devised from these interactions.

Strengthened Relationships

When you listen effectively, free from bias, you deposit trust and respect into your relational bank accounts. These investments pay off by building stronger, more resilient connections. People feel valued when they are truly heard, which can turn ordinary interactions into robust, lasting relationships.

By mastering the skill of listening beyond bias, you become not just a participant in conversations but a maestro, orchestrating a symphony of genuine dialogue and mutual understanding. This chapter emphasizes how refining your listening skills can elevate your communication to new heights, creating richer, more meaningful interactions.

CHAPTER 5

Always Communicate with the End Goal in Mind

Communication is one of the most essential skills in life, yet it is often overlooked in terms of its complexity and impact. Effective communication is not just about exchanging information; it's about understanding the emotions and intentions behind the information. In any relationship—whether with friends, colleagues, or a significant other—having clear and purposeful communication can strengthen bonds, resolve conflicts, and foster mutual understanding. Knowing your end goal when communicating ensures that you convey your message effectively and meaningfully.

Setting the Destination

The first step to effective communication is understanding your purpose. Why are you engaging in this conversation? Are you trying to share information, resolve a conflict, give instructions, or simply express your feelings? Understanding your purpose helps you stay focused and ensures that your message is clear.

For instance, if you're discussing weekend plans with your friends, your goal might be to come to a mutual agreement on what to do. You'll need to be clear about your suggestions and open to hearing theirs. If you're having a performance review with a colleague, your goal is to provide constructive feedback and help them improve. Your communication should be supportive and specific. In a relationship, when discussing future plans, the goal might be to ensure both partners are on the same page and feel valued and heard.

By clearly defining your purpose, you avoid misunderstandings and keep the conversation on track. This clarity is especially important in relationships, where miscommunication can lead to frustration and conflict. Understanding your goal allows you to tailor your message to your audience, ensuring that it resonates and achieves the desired outcome.

Choosing the Right Method

Effective communication involves selecting the appropriate method to convey your message. Different situations and relationships call for different approaches.

Verbal Communication: Speaking directly to someone allows for immediate feedback and clarification. It is ideal for situations that require a quick response or when discussing sensitive issues. Ensure your words are clear and your tone matches your message. In friendships, verbal communication is crucial for expressing emotions and building trust. For example, if you're upset with a friend, discussing it in person can help resolve the issue more effectively than a text message.

Nonverbal Communication: Body language, facial expressions, and gestures can significantly impact how your message is received. Nonverbal cues can reinforce what you're saying or convey emotions that words cannot. In relationships, a reassuring touch or a warm smile can communicate affection and support without needing words. Being mindful of your nonverbal signals ensures that your message is consistent and clear. Misaligned nonverbal communication can lead to misunderstandings, as people often trust nonverbal cues more than spoken words.

Written Communication: Emails, texts, and letters are excellent for providing detailed information or when documentation is necessary. Written communication allows the recipient to process the information at their own pace. In a professional setting, clear and concise emails can prevent misunderstandings and keep projects on track. In personal relationships, a thoughtful letter or message can convey deep feelings and appreciation that may be hard to express verbally. Writing also gives you the chance to think carefully about your words, reducing the risk of miscommunication.

Visual Communication: Using visuals such as charts, graphs, or videos can help explain complex ideas more clearly. Visual aids can make abstract concepts more tangible and easier to understand. In a work context, presentations with visuals can help illustrate your points more effectively. In personal relationships, sharing photos or videos can create shared memories and enhance your connection. Visuals can also help bridge language barriers, making your message accessible to a wider audience.

Choosing the right method ensures that your message is delivered in the most effective way possible. It shows respect for the preferences and needs of the person you're communicating with, whether it's a friend, colleague, or partner. Tailoring your communication style to the situation and the audience increases the likelihood that your message will be understood and appreciated.

Avoiding Misunderstandings

Misunderstandings are common in communication, but they can be minimized by being clear and checking for understanding. It's essential to ensure that the person you're communicating with fully comprehends your message.

Ask questions like, "Does that make sense?" or "Do you have any questions?" to check for understanding. This is especially important in professional settings, where misunderstandings can lead to mistakes or delays. In personal relationships, clarifying your message can prevent conflicts and ensure that both parties feel heard and understood. Active listening is another critical component. When someone else is speaking, give them your full attention. This means not only hearing their words but also observing their nonverbal cues and understanding their emotions. Active listening shows that you value their input and are engaged in the conversation. It also helps you respond more appropriately and effectively. Reflecting back what the other person has said, by summarizing or paraphrasing, can also confirm understanding and show that you are truly listening.

Misunderstandings often arise from assumptions and incomplete information. To avoid these pitfalls, make your intentions and expectations clear from the beginning. This proactive approach can prevent confusion and keep the communication process smooth. Additionally, be mindful of cultural and individual differences in communication styles. What seems clear to you might be interpreted differently by someone with a different background or experience. Awareness of these differences can help you adjust your communication style to be more effective.

In relationships, misunderstandings can be particularly damaging. They can lead to feelings of frustration, resentment, and disconnection. By actively seeking to avoid detours and roadblocks, you show your partner that you care about their feelings and are committed to maintaining a clear and open line of communication. This is also important in friendships, where clarity and understanding are the foundations of a strong bond. Regularly checking in and clarifying points can prevent small misunderstandings from growing into larger issues.

The Value of Thinking Before You Speak

In the rush of everyday life, it's easy to blurt out the first thing that comes to mind. However, taking a moment to think before you speak can drastically improve the quality of your communication. Reflecting on your words and their potential impact ensures that you convey your message thoughtfully and respectfully.

Pausing to consider your words allows you to align your message with your end goal. Ask yourself, "What am I trying to achieve with this conversation?" and "How can I say this in a way that will be most effective?" This brief moment of reflection can prevent misunderstandings and reduce the likelihood of saying something you might regret. It shows that you are intentional about your communication and considerate of the other person's feelings.

Taking a breather before speaking can also help you manage your emotions. If you're feeling angry or upset, a short pause allows you to calm down and approach the conversation more rationally. This can prevent heated arguments and ensure that the discussion remains productive. In relationships, this pause can be the difference between a constructive conversation and a damaging confrontation. It demonstrates emotional intelligence and self-control, which are crucial for maintaining healthy relationships.

Remember, it's perfectly okay to take your time before responding. You can say, "Let me think about that for a moment," or "I need a minute to gather my thoughts." This not only gives you time to formulate a clear and thoughtful response but also shows the other person that you are taking the conversation seriously. In professional settings, taking time to think before you speak can lead to more measured and effective communication, reducing the risk of misunderstandings and mistakes.

Adapting Your Approach

Flexibility in communication is vital. Not every conversation will go as planned, and you may need to adapt your approach. If the other person isn't understanding your message, try explaining it differently. Use simpler language, provide examples, or use visual aids.

Adapting your approach shows that you are attentive to the other person's needs and willing to adjust to ensure they understand. This is particularly important in professional settings, where clear communication is essential for collaboration and productivity. For example, if a colleague doesn't grasp a concept during a meeting, following up with an email that includes detailed instructions and visuals can help. Adaptability demonstrates your commitment to achieving mutual understanding and success.

In personal relationships, being adaptable can prevent conflicts and show that you respect your partner's perspective. If your partner doesn't respond well to direct criticism, you might find a more gentle and supportive way to express your concerns. Flexibility in communication demonstrates empathy and a willingness to find common ground. It shows that you are not rigid in your approach and are considerate of your partner's feelings and viewpoints.

Being adaptable also means being open to changing your mind and approach based on new information or feedback. This openness fosters a collaborative environment where both parties feel valued and understood. In friendships, flexibility and understanding can prevent conflicts and strengthen the bond of trust. It shows that you are willing to make adjustments for the sake of the relationship, which can lead to deeper and more meaningful connections.

The Role of Feedback

Feedback is a powerful tool in communication. It helps you understand how your message was received and whether any adjustments are needed. Encouraging feedback by asking questions like, "What do you think?" or "How do you feel about this?" shows that you value the other person's opinion.

Listening to feedback allows you to improve your communication skills and build stronger relationships. It also helps to clarify any misunderstandings and ensure that your message is understood as intended. In professional settings, constructive feedback can enhance team performance and foster a collaborative environment. Regular feedback sessions can help identify areas for improvement and celebrate successes.

In personal relationships, feedback is essential for growth and mutual understanding. It allows both partners to express their needs, concerns, and appreciations openly. By fostering an environment where feedback is welcomed and respected, you build a stronger foundation of trust and mutual respect. In friendships, feedback helps to resolve issues and strengthens the relationship by showing that you care about your friend's feelings and perspectives.

Feedback should be specific, focused on behaviors rather than personal attributes, and delivered with the intention of fostering improvement. Constructive feedback can lead to positive changes and personal growth, while also strengthening the relationship by demonstrating care and commitment. It's important to be receptive to feedback and to use it as an opportunity to learn and improve your communication skills.

Celebrating Success

When you achieve your communication goal, it's important to acknowledge and celebrate the success. This reinforces the importance of clear and purposeful communication and encourages continued effort and improvement.

Celebrating communication successes can be as simple as expressing gratitude and acknowledging the achievement. In professional settings, recognizing team efforts can boost morale and motivation. Celebrations can be formal, such as awards and ceremonies, or informal, like a team lunch or a thank-you note. In personal relationships, celebrating milestones together creates lasting memories and deepens the bond. Recognizing and appreciating each other's efforts fosters a sense of partnership and mutual respect.

Recognizing and celebrating milestones, no matter how small, can boost morale and motivation. It's a reminder that effective communication is a journey, and each successful interaction is a step towards mastering this vital skill. Celebrating these moments helps build a positive and supportive environment, whether in the workplace or in personal relationships.

In relationships, celebrating communication successes can strengthen your bond. Whether it's resolving a conflict, making a joint decision, or simply having a meaningful conversation, taking the time to acknowledge and appreciate these moments fosters a deeper connection and reinforces your commitment to each other. In friendships, celebrating milestones together creates lasting memories and deepens the friendship. It shows that you value and appreciate the relationship and the efforts made to maintain it.

The Power of Purposeful Communication

Always communicating with the end goal in mind ensures that your interactions are meaningful and effective. By understanding your purpose, choosing the right method, avoiding misunderstandings, adapting your approach, and seeking feedback, you can navigate any conversation successfully. Remember, flexibility and adaptability are key to effective communication. Celebrating your successes reinforces the importance of clear and purposeful communication and strengthens your relationships.

In relationships, purposeful communication can transform your interactions. It builds trust, fosters understanding, and strengthens your bond. Taking the time to think before you speak can prevent misunderstandings and enhance the quality of your communication. So, next time you start a conversation, think about where you want to go. Set your communication goal, choose your method, and navigate with confidence. With the end goal in mind, you'll always find your way, and your relationships will flourish.

CHAPTER 6

Overcoming Emotional Communication: Mastering Your Emotions

Emotions are a natural and integral part of human experience, influencing our thoughts, actions, and interactions. However, when it comes to communication, especially in uncomfortable situations, allowing emotions to control how you speak can lead to misunderstandings, conflicts, and regrets. Learning to manage your emotions effectively can enhance your communication skills, foster better relationships, and lead to more constructive outcomes. This chapter will provide detailed strategies, tips, and real-time examples to help you communicate effectively without letting your emotions take the reins.

Understanding Emotional Communication

Emotional communication occurs when your feelings heavily influence the way you express yourself. While emotions can add depth and authenticity to your communication, they can also cloud your judgment, leading to impulsive reactions or words you might later regret. Recognizing when your emotions are taking over is the first step to managing them effectively.

Consider a scenario where a colleague criticizes your work in a meeting. If your initial reaction is anger, you might respond defensively or aggressively, escalating the situation. However, if you manage to control your emotional response, you can address the criticism constructively, maintaining a professional demeanor and potentially learning from the feedback. Here are seven tips that can really help.

1. Pause and Breathe

When faced with an emotional trigger, take a moment to pause and breathe deeply. This simple technique can help calm your nervous system and give you a moment to collect your thoughts before responding. Deep breathing activates the parasympathetic nervous system, which helps reduce stress and promotes relaxation.

Pausing and breathing not only calms your mind but also provides a brief window to think before you speak. This pause can prevent impulsive reactions that you might later regret. It's especially useful in heated arguments or when you feel overwhelmed by strong emotions. Practicing this regularly can help make it a natural response in stressful situations.

Example: During a heated argument with a friend, instead of immediately lashing out, take a deep breath and count to ten. This pause can help you respond more thoughtfully and avoid saying something you might regret.

2. Acknowledge Your Emotions

Recognizing and acknowledging your emotions can help you gain control over them. Instead of suppressing your feelings, accept them and understand why you feel the way you do. This self-awareness can prevent emotions from bubbling up uncontrollably and affecting your communication.

Acknowledging your emotions involves naming them and understanding their root causes. Are you feeling angry because you feel disrespected? Are you anxious because you fear failure? Understanding the underlying reasons for your emotions can help you address them more effectively. This introspection also allows you to communicate your feelings more clearly and constructively.

Example: If you feel hurt by a partner's comment, silently acknowledge, "I am feeling hurt because that comment made me feel undervalued." This awareness allows you to address your feelings without letting them dominate the conversation.

3. Use "I" Statements

"I" statements focus on your feelings and experiences rather than blaming or criticizing the other person. This approach can reduce defensiveness and promote constructive dialogue. By owning your emotions and experiences, you create a space for open and honest communication without making the other person feel attacked.

Using "I" statements involves structuring your sentences to reflect your feelings and needs.

For example, instead of saying, "You never listen to me," which can come across as accusatory, you might say, "I feel unheard when I'm interrupted." This subtle shift in language helps the other person understand your perspective without feeling blamed, paving the way for a more empathetic and productive conversation.

Example: Instead of saying, "You never listen to me," try, "I feel unheard when I'm interrupted." This shifts the focus to your experience and opens the door for a more empathetic conversation.

4. Practice Active Listening

Active listening involves fully concentrating on what the other person is saying, understanding their message, and responding thoughtfully. This practice can help you stay calm and engaged, rather than reacting impulsively. Active listening shows respect and empathy, fostering a deeper connection and understanding.

To practice active listening, focus on the speaker without interrupting. Reflect back what you've heard by summarizing or paraphrasing their words. This not only confirms that you understand their message but also shows that you value their input. Maintaining eye contact, nodding, and using verbal affirmations like "I see" or "I understand" can also enhance active listening.

Example: In a disagreement with a colleague, make a conscious effort to listen to their point of view without interrupting. Repeat back what they've said to confirm understanding before sharing your perspective.

5. Take a Break if Needed

If emotions are too intense, it's okay to take a break from the conversation. Stepping away for a few minutes can help you cool down and approach the discussion with a clearer mind. This break can prevent escalation and give both parties time to reflect on their thoughts and feelings.

Taking a break doesn't mean avoiding the conversation altogether. It's about giving yourself the space to calm down and return to the discussion with a more composed and rational mindset. Communicate your need for a break to the other person respectfully, ensuring they understand that you intend to continue the conversation once you've collected your thoughts.

Example: In the middle of a family argument, you might say, "I need a few minutes to calm down. Can we take a break and continue this conversation later?" This allows you to regain composure and prevent the situation from escalating.

6. Reframe Negative Thoughts

Negative emotions often stem from negative thoughts. Reframing these thoughts can help you view the situation more positively and respond more constructively. Cognitive reframing involves changing your perspective on a situation to alter its emotional impact.

To reframe negative thoughts, challenge the assumptions behind them. Instead of thinking, "They're attacking me personally," consider, "They have a different perspective that I need to understand." This shift in mindset can reduce emotional intensity and foster a more open dialogue. Practicing gratitude and focusing on positive aspects can also help reframe negative thoughts.

Example: Instead of thinking, "They're attacking me personally," reframe it to, "They have a different perspective that I need to understand." This shift in mindset can reduce emotional intensity and foster a more open dialogue.

7. Practice Mindfulness and Self-Regulation

Mindfulness involves being present and aware of your thoughts and feelings without judgment. Regular mindfulness practice can improve emotional regulation and help you stay calm under pressure. Mindfulness techniques, such as meditation and deep breathing, can enhance your ability to manage stress and maintain emotional balance.

Self-regulation is the ability to control your emotional responses and behaviors. Developing self-regulation skills involves recognizing your emotional triggers and implementing strategies to manage them. Techniques like progressive muscle relaxation, visualization, and journaling can help you develop better self-regulation skills.

Example: Before a stressful meeting, spend a few minutes practicing mindfulness meditation. Focus on your breath and let go of any distracting thoughts. This can help you enter the meeting with a calm and centered mindset.

Real-Time Examples of Managing Emotions in Conversations

Example 1: Managing Anger in a Professional Setting

Scenario: You receive harsh criticism from your boss in front of your team.

Emotional Reaction: Anger and embarrassment.

Controlled Response:

1. **Pause and Breathe:** Take a deep breath to calm your immediate reaction.
2. **Acknowledge Your Emotions:** Internally note that you feel angry and embarrassed.
3. **Use "I" Statements:** Later, approach your boss privately and say, "I felt embarrassed when my work was criticized in front of the team. Can we

discuss feedback in a one-on-one setting in the future?"
4. **Reframe Negative Thoughts:** Instead of thinking, "My boss hates me," reframe it to, "My boss is trying to help me improve."

Example 2: Handling Frustration in a Personal Relationship

Scenario: Your partner forgets an important anniversary.

Emotional Reaction: Frustration and disappointment.

Controlled Response:

1. **Take a Break:** If you're too upset to talk, take a few minutes to cool down.
2. **Acknowledge Your Emotions:** Recognize your disappointment and frustration.

3. **Use "I" Statements:** When you're ready, say, "I felt really disappointed when our anniversary was forgotten. Can we talk about how to avoid this in the future?"
4. **Practice Active Listening:** Listen to your partner's response without interrupting to understand their perspective.

Example 3: Navigating Anxiety in a Social Situation

Scenario: You're anxious about giving a presentation at work.

Emotional Reaction: Anxiety and fear.

Controlled Response:

1. **Practice Mindfulness:** Spend a few minutes before the presentation focusing on your breath and calming your mind.

2. **Reframe Negative Thoughts:** Change "I'm going to mess up" to "I'm prepared and capable of doing well."
3. **Pause and Breathe:** During the presentation, if you feel overwhelmed, take a brief pause, breathe, and then continue.
4. **Acknowledge Your Emotions:** After the presentation, reflect on your anxiety and consider what strategies helped you manage it.

Building Long-Term Emotional Regulation Skills

Regular Mindfulness Practice

Engage in daily mindfulness or meditation practices to improve overall emotional regulation. This can help you stay grounded and less reactive in stressful situations. Mindfulness can be practiced through meditation, yoga, or simply paying attention to your breath and surroundings.

Developing a consistent mindfulness practice can increase your emotional awareness and resilience. Over time, mindfulness can help you respond to emotional triggers with greater calm and clarity, reducing the likelihood of impulsive reactions. Incorporating mindfulness into your daily routine can also enhance your overall well-being and reduce stress.

Develop Emotional Awareness

Regularly reflect on your emotional responses and identify patterns. Understanding your emotional triggers can help you prepare for and manage them more effectively. Keep a journal to track your emotions and the situations that trigger them, noting any patterns or recurring themes.

Emotional awareness involves recognizing not only your emotions but also the physical sensations and thoughts associated with them. This awareness can help you catch emotional reactions early and implement strategies to manage them before they escalate. Developing emotional awareness can improve your self-regulation and enhance your communication skills.

Seek Feedback

Ask trusted friends or colleagues for feedback on how you handle emotional situations. Constructive feedback can provide insights and help you improve your emotional regulation skills. Be open to hearing others' perspectives and use their feedback to identify areas for improvement.

Regularly seeking feedback can help you stay accountable and committed to your personal growth. It can also strengthen your relationships by showing that you value others' opinions and are willing to make changes to improve your interactions. Use feedback as an opportunity to learn and grow, both personally and professionally.

Professional Development

Consider attending workshops or seeking professional coaching on emotional intelligence and communication. These resources can offer valuable tools and techniques for managing emotions effectively. Professional development can provide structured learning opportunities and support your journey toward better emotional regulation.

Investing in professional development can enhance your skills and confidence, making you more effective in both personal and professional interactions. Look for courses, seminars, or coaching programs that focus on emotional intelligence, conflict resolution, and effective communication. Continuing education can help you stay current with best practices and deepen your understanding of emotional regulation.

Healthy Lifestyle Choices

Maintain a healthy lifestyle through regular exercise, balanced nutrition, and adequate sleep. Physical well-being significantly impacts emotional stability and resilience. Regular exercise can reduce stress, improve mood, and increase energy levels, while a balanced diet and sufficient sleep support overall health and well-being.

Healthy lifestyle choices can enhance your ability to manage stress and regulate emotions. Prioritizing self-care can help you build resilience and maintain emotional balance, even in challenging situations. Incorporating healthy habits into your daily routine can improve your physical, emotional, and mental health, contributing to better overall well-being.

Talk Less, Communicate More!

Mastering Emotional Communication

Effective communication, especially in uncomfortable situations, requires mastery over your emotions. By pausing and breathing, acknowledging your emotions, using "I" statements, practicing active listening, taking breaks, reframing negative thoughts, and practicing mindfulness, you can manage your emotional responses and communicate more effectively. Over time, developing these skills will enhance your relationships, both personal and professional, and lead to more constructive and meaningful interactions.

Remember, it's natural to feel emotions strongly, but how you manage and express them defines your communication success. By not allowing your emotions to control the way you speak, you can ensure that your message is clear, respectful, and conducive to positive outcomes. Practicing these strategies consistently can help you build emotional resilience and improve your communication skills, leading to stronger relationships and more effective

CHAPTER 7

The Courage to Communicate

Courage is the foundation upon which effective communication is built. No matter how many techniques or tips you learn, they are rendered useless if you lack the courage to open your mouth and speak. The courage to communicate is not just about speaking out loud; it's about expressing your true thoughts, feelings, and ideas despite the fear of judgment or rejection. In this chapter, we will delve into the importance of courage in communication, the barriers that prevent us from speaking up, and practical strategies to build and harness this courage.

The Importance of Courage in Communication

Courage in communication is essential for several reasons. First and foremost, it allows for authentic interactions. When you have the courage to communicate honestly, you present your true self to others. This authenticity fosters trust and builds stronger relationships, whether in personal or professional settings. Without courage, conversations often remain superficial, as we hide behind what we think others want to hear rather than what we truly believe or feel. This superficiality can lead to misunderstandings and a lack of genuine connection, preventing the development of deep, meaningful relationships.

Secondly, courage in communication is critical for personal growth and development. When you express your ideas and opinions, you open yourself up to feedback and new perspectives. This exchange is vital for learning and self-improvement. Fearful silence, on the other hand, keeps you stagnant and prevents you from growing. Courage enables you to step out of your comfort zone, take risks, and embrace the unknown, all of which are necessary for continuous personal development. By speaking up and engaging in open dialogue, you challenge yourself and others, leading to a more dynamic and enriching life experience.

Lastly, courage is essential for driving change. Whether it's standing up for what's right, challenging the status quo, or proposing innovative ideas, courageous communication is often the catalyst for significant changes. History is filled with examples of individuals who had the courage to speak up and, as a result, made a substantial impact. From civil rights leaders to innovative entrepreneurs, these individuals did not allow the fear of judgment or rejection to silence them. Without courage, important issues remain unaddressed, and progress is hindered. Courageous communication empowers individuals and communities to advocate for change and improvement, driving societal advancement and innovation.

Barriers to Courageous Communication

Several barriers can prevent us from communicating courageously. Understanding these barriers is the first step towards overcoming them.

Fear of Judgment

One of the most common barriers is the fear of judgment. We worry about what others will think or say about us, fearing that we will be criticized or ridiculed. This fear can be paralyzing and prevent us from expressing our true thoughts and feelings. It's important to recognize that this fear often stems from past experiences and is not necessarily reflective of the present situation. By acknowledging and addressing these past experiences, we can begin to separate them from our current reality and reduce their impact on our communication.

Moreover, the fear of judgment can be exacerbated by societal norms and expectations. We often feel pressured to conform to certain standards or behaviors to be accepted by our peers or society at large. This pressure can lead us to suppress our true selves and communicate in ways that we believe will be more socially acceptable. However, this inauthentic communication can prevent us from forming genuine connections and hinder our personal growth. To overcome this barrier, it is essential to challenge societal norms and embrace our unique perspectives and identities.

Fear of Rejection

Closely related to the fear of judgment is the fear of rejection. We fear that by speaking up, we might be rejected or excluded by our peers. This fear is particularly strong in social and professional settings where acceptance and belonging are highly valued. The fear of rejection can lead us to conform to others' expectations rather than voicing our own opinions. By doing so, we lose our individuality and compromise our integrity. It's important to recognize that rejection is a natural part of life and does not define our worth or value.

Rejection can also be an opportunity for growth and learning. When we face rejection, we are given the chance to reflect on our communication and consider how we can improve. Instead of seeing rejection as a failure, we can view it as a stepping stone towards better understanding and stronger relationships. By embracing rejection and learning from it, we can build resilience and develop a more courageous approach to communication.

Low Self-Esteem

Low self-esteem can also be a significant barrier to courageous communication. When we lack confidence in our abilities or the value of our contributions, we are less likely to speak up. This lack of self-belief can be deeply ingrained and challenging to overcome, but it's essential to work on building self-esteem to communicate effectively. One way to build self-esteem is to focus on your strengths and achievements, recognizing the unique qualities and skills you bring to the table.

Building self-esteem also involves challenging negative self-talk and replacing it with positive affirmations. Instead of focusing on your perceived flaws or weaknesses, remind yourself of your worth and the value of your contributions. Seek support from trusted friends, family members, or mentors who can provide encouragement and help you build your confidence. By fostering a positive self-image, you can develop the courage to communicate more openly and authentically.

Perfectionism

Perfectionism is another barrier that can inhibit courageous communication. The desire to communicate perfectly can lead to overthinking and hesitation. We might wait until we feel we have the perfect words or the perfect timing, which can result in missed opportunities. It's important to remember that effective communication is not about perfection but about authenticity and clarity. Striving for perfection can create unrealistic expectations and increase anxiety, making it difficult to communicate confidently.

To overcome perfectionism, it's essential to embrace imperfection and understand that making mistakes is a natural part of the learning process. Instead of aiming for flawless communication, focus on being clear and genuine in your interactions. Accept that there will be times when you might stumble or say something imperfectly, and that's okay. By letting go of the need for perfection, you can communicate more freely and courageously.

Building the Courage to Communicate

Building the courage to communicate takes time and effort, but it's a crucial step towards becoming an effective communicator. Here are some strategies to help you build and harness this courage.

Recognize and Challenge Your Fears

The first step in building courage is to recognize and challenge your fears. Take some time to reflect on what specifically you are afraid of when it comes to communication. Is it the fear of judgment, rejection, or failure? Once you have identified your fears, challenge them by asking yourself if they are rational and based on facts. Often, our fears are exaggerated and not reflective of reality. By questioning the validity of your fears, you can begin to diminish their power over you.

Another effective way to challenge your fears is through exposure. Gradually expose yourself to situations that trigger your fear of communication. Start with low-stakes scenarios and work your way up to more challenging ones. This gradual exposure can help desensitize you to the fear and build your confidence. Remember, the goal is not to eliminate fear completely but to learn how to manage it and not let it control your actions.

Start Small

Building courage doesn't happen overnight. Start by practicing courageous communication in low-stakes situations. This could be as simple as sharing your opinion in a casual conversation with a friend or asking a question in a small group setting. These small steps can help build your confidence and prepare you for more challenging situations. As you become more comfortable speaking up in these smaller settings, you can gradually take on more significant communication challenges.

Additionally, starting small allows you to experience positive outcomes from your communication efforts. These positive experiences can reinforce your confidence and encourage you to continue speaking up. Celebrate your successes, no matter how small they may seem, and use them as motivation to keep pushing yourself. Over time, these incremental steps will accumulate, leading to greater courage and more effective communication.

Focus on the Positive Outcomes

Instead of focusing on what could go wrong, shift your attention to the positive outcomes of courageous communication. Think about the benefits of speaking up, such as gaining new insights, building stronger relationships, and driving positive change. Visualizing these positive outcomes can help reduce anxiety and build courage. By focusing on the potential rewards rather than the risks, you can approach communication with a more positive and proactive mindset.

Another way to focus on positive outcomes is to set clear and achievable communication goals. For example, you might set a goal to contribute at least one idea during a team meeting or to share a personal story with a friend. By setting and achieving these goals, you can experience the positive impact of your communication efforts firsthand. This success can further reinforce your courage and motivate you to continue speaking up.

Prepare and Practice

Preparation can significantly boost your confidence and courage. If you need to communicate something important, take the time to prepare and practice what you want to say. This could involve writing down your thoughts, rehearsing with a trusted friend, or practicing in front of a mirror. The more prepared you are, the more confident and courageous you will feel. Preparation helps you organize your thoughts, anticipate potential questions or challenges, and refine your message for clarity and impact.

In addition to preparation, regular practice is essential for building communication skills and confidence. Seek out opportunities to practice speaking in various settings, such as public speaking clubs, workshops, or social gatherings. The more you practice, the more comfortable and confident you will become in expressing yourself. Practice also allows you to learn from your experiences, make adjustments, and improve your communication over time.

Embrace Imperfection

It's important to remember that communication doesn't have to be perfect. Embrace imperfection and understand that it's okay to make mistakes. What matters most is that you are honest and authentic in your communication. Over time, you will become more comfortable with the idea of imperfection, which will help build your courage. Recognize that even the most effective communicators have moments of uncertainty and imperfection, and that's a normal part of the process.

By accepting imperfection, you can reduce the pressure you place on yourself and communicate more freely. Instead of striving for flawless delivery, focus on conveying your message clearly and sincerely. Be kind to yourself and view mistakes as opportunities for growth and learning. This mindset shift can help you approach communication with greater confidence and resilience.

Seek Support

Surround yourself with supportive people who encourage and uplift you. Having a strong support system can make a significant difference in building your courage to communicate. Seek out friends, family members, or mentors who can provide positive feedback and help you build your confidence. Their encouragement and belief in your abilities can bolster your self-esteem and motivate you to keep pushing yourself.

In addition to personal support networks, consider joining groups or communities that focus on improving communication skills. Public speaking clubs, such as Toastmasters, offer a supportive environment for practicing and honing your communication abilities. These groups provide constructive feedback, camaraderie, and opportunities to practice in a safe and encouraging setting. Engaging with others who share similar goals can be motivating and empowering.

Reflect on Past Successes

Reflecting on past successes can also help build your courage. Think about times when you communicated courageously and the positive outcomes that resulted. Reminding yourself of these successes can boost your confidence and encourage you to continue speaking up. Keep a journal of your communication achievements and revisit it when you need a confidence boost. These reflections can serve as a reminder of your capabilities and the positive impact of your courageous efforts.

Additionally, seek feedback from others about your communication strengths. Ask trusted friends, colleagues, or mentors to share their observations of your effective communication moments. Their positive feedback can reinforce your confidence and provide valuable insights into your strengths. By acknowledging and celebrating your successes, you can build a solid foundation of self-belief that supports courageous communication.

The Power of Being Vulnerable

Owning our vulnerabilities is a powerful aspect of courageous communication. Vulnerability is often seen as a weakness, but in reality, it is a strength that fosters genuine connections and trust. When we are vulnerable, we open ourselves up to others, showing them our true selves. This openness encourages others to do the same, creating an environment of mutual trust and understanding. In personal relationships, vulnerability can lead to deeper and more meaningful connections. By sharing our fears, insecurities, and emotions, we allow others to see us for who we truly are, fostering empathy and compassion.

In professional settings, vulnerability can enhance teamwork and collaboration. When leaders show vulnerability, they create a safe space for their team members to express their ideas and concerns without fear of judgment. This openness can lead to more innovative solutions and a stronger team dynamic. Owning our vulnerabilities also means acknowledging our mistakes and learning from them. This humility and willingness to grow can inspire others to do the same, creating a culture of continuous improvement and mutual respect.

Embracing vulnerability requires courage. It means letting go of the fear of being judged or rejected and trusting that being authentic will lead to positive outcomes. This trust is essential for building strong and resilient relationships. When we hide our vulnerabilities, we create a façade that can prevent others from truly connecting with us. By contrast, when we embrace and share our vulnerabilities, we invite others to do the same, leading to more honest and fulfilling interactions. Owning our vulnerabilities is not about seeking pity or sympathy; it's about being real and authentic in our interactions, which ultimately leads to stronger and more meaningful connections.

Furthermore, vulnerability allows us to build deeper self-awareness and self-acceptance. When we acknowledge and embrace our vulnerabilities, we are accepting all parts of ourselves, not just the polished and presentable aspects. This self-acceptance is crucial for building self-esteem and confidence. By being comfortable with our vulnerabilities, we become more resilient and less affected by external judgments. We learn to trust ourselves and our abilities, which in turn empowers us to communicate more openly and courageously.

Practical Tips for Courageous Communication

Here are some practical tips to help you communicate courageously in various situations:

In Personal Relationships

- **Be Honest and Open:** In personal relationships, honesty and openness are

Talk Less, Communicate More!

key. Share your true thoughts and feelings with your partner, family, and friends. This builds trust and strengthens your relationships. When you communicate honestly, you create a foundation of trust that allows for deeper and more meaningful connections.

- **Express Your Needs:** Don't be afraid to express your needs and desires. Communicating your needs clearly can prevent misunderstandings and ensure that your needs are met. It's important to remember that your needs are valid, and expressing them is essential for maintaining healthy and balanced relationships.

- **Set Boundaries:** Setting boundaries is an important aspect of courageous communication. Don't be afraid to say no or communicate your limits. Establishing boundaries helps protect your well-being and ensures that your relationships are respectful and supportive.

In Professional Settings

- Speak Up in Meetings: Practice speaking up in meetings, even if it's just to ask a question or share a brief comment. This can help build your confidence and establish your presence. Contributing to discussions demonstrates your engagement and commitment to the team.
- Share Your Ideas: Don't hesitate to share your ideas and suggestions. Remember that your perspective is valuable, and your contributions can make a difference. Innovative ideas and fresh perspectives can drive progress and improvement within your organization.

- Seek Feedback: Actively seek feedback from colleagues and supervisors. This shows that you are open to learning and improving, and it can help build your confidence. Constructive feedback provides valuable insights and helps you grow as a communicator and professional.

The Importance of Putting in the Work

Building the courage to communicate effectively requires dedication and consistent effort. At first, the journey might feel daunting and uncomfortable. Stepping out of your comfort zone to express your true thoughts and feelings can be challenging, especially if you have long-standing fears of judgment or rejection. However, it is essential to remember that growth and improvement come from persistent practice and determination. Just like learning any new skill, developing the courage to communicate takes time and effort, but the rewards are well worth it.

Initially, you might encounter setbacks and moments of self-doubt. You may find yourself struggling with anxiety or second-guessing your words. These challenges are a natural part of the process and should not discourage you. Embrace these experiences as opportunities to learn and grow. Each time you push through your discomfort and speak up, you are building resilience and reinforcing your ability to communicate courageously. Over time, these efforts will accumulate, leading to increased confidence and a greater sense of ease in expressing yourself.

As you continue to put in the work, you will notice that what once seemed difficult becomes more manageable. The practice of speaking up and being vulnerable will start to feel more natural. You will become more adept at handling your fears and anxieties, and your communication will become more fluid and authentic. This transformation does not happen overnight, but with consistent effort and perseverance, it will happen. The key is to remain patient and committed to the process. By continuously challenging yourself and embracing the discomfort, you will develop the courage and skills needed to communicate effectively in any situation.

The courage to communicate is the cornerstone of effective communication. Without it, no amount of tips or techniques will be useful. By recognizing and challenging your fears, starting small, focusing on positive outcomes, preparing and practicing, embracing imperfection, seeking support, and reflecting on past successes, you can build and harness the courage to communicate. Remember, it's not about being perfect; it's about being authentic and true to yourself. Every time you speak up, you are taking a step towards becoming a more confident and effective communicator. Don't let fear hold you back. Embrace the courage to communicate, and watch as your relationships, personal growth, and ability to effect change flourish.

www.ingramcontent.com/pod-product-compliance
Lightning Source LLC
Chambersburg PA
CBHW071511150426
43191CB00009B/1490